I Can Read!

READING 2 WITH HELP

AFTER THE DINOSAURS

Mammoths and Fossil Mammals

written by **Charlotte Lewis Brown**   pictures by **Phil Wilson**

HarperCollins*Publishers*

This book is dedicated with gratitude
to the teachers of the Los Angeles public schools
who made and are making a difference
(and especially to those from Anchorage Elementary
and Coeur d'Alene Elementary)
—C.L.B.

To my parents, for their love and support,
and to Mr. William G. Applequist,
my high school art teacher, with gratitude
—P.W.

After the Dinosaurs: Mammoths and Fossil Mammals Text copyright © 2006 by Kathryn Ann Hoppe Illustrations copyright © 2006 by Phil Wilson All rights reserved. No part of this book may be used or reproduced in any manner whatsoever without written permission except in the case of brief quotations embodied in critical articles and reviews. Printed in the United States of America. For information address HarperCollins Children's Books, a division of HarperCollins Publishers, 1350 Avenue of the Americas, New York, NY 10019. www.harperchildrens.com

Library of Congress Cataloging-in-Publication Data

Brown, Charlotte Lewis.
  After the dinosaurs : mammoths and fossil mammals / by Charlotte Lewis Brown, pictures by Phil Wilson.
    p.   cm. — (I can read book)
  ISBN-10: 0-06-053053-7 (trade bdg) — ISBN-13: 978-0-06-053053-2 (trade bdg)
  ISBN-10: 0-06-053054-5 (lib bdg) — ISBN-13: 978-0-06-053054-9 (lib bdg)
  1. Mammals, Fossil—Juvenile literature. I. Title. II. Series.
QE881.B84 2006   2005028662
569—dc22   CIP
                                                                            AC

1 2 3 4 5 6 7 8 9 10 ❖   First Edition

CONTENTS

Long, long ago,
dinosaurs lived everywhere,
but they were not alone.
Small, furry animals
called mammals
lived with the dinosaurs.

The mammals were different
from the dinosaurs.

The mammals were very small.
Instead of scaly skin,
the mammals had hair.
Mother mammals fed
their babies milk.
Mother dinosaurs did not.

Dinosaurs and mammals lived
together for millions of years.
The dinosaurs grew bigger
and bigger.
But the mammals stayed small.
When the dinosaurs died,
the mammals survived.
Millions of years passed.
The mammals grew larger.
Some of these mammals
looked like animals alive today.
And some of these mammals
looked very strange!

WOOLLY MAMMOTH

You say it like this:

WOOL-ee MAM-uth

Woolly mammoths looked
like hairy elephants.
They lived where it was very cold.
They used their big tusks
to dig under the snow
to get grass to eat.
Sometimes mammoths froze
to death under the snow.

n very cold places, such as Alaska,
people sometimes find
mammoths still frozen today.

SMILODON

You say it like this:
SMILE-oh-don

Smilodon is also called
a "saber-toothed tiger."

Its teeth were as sharp as knives
and longer than your hand.
It ate meat.
It hid until an animal came close.
Then it jumped on the animal—
and ate it!

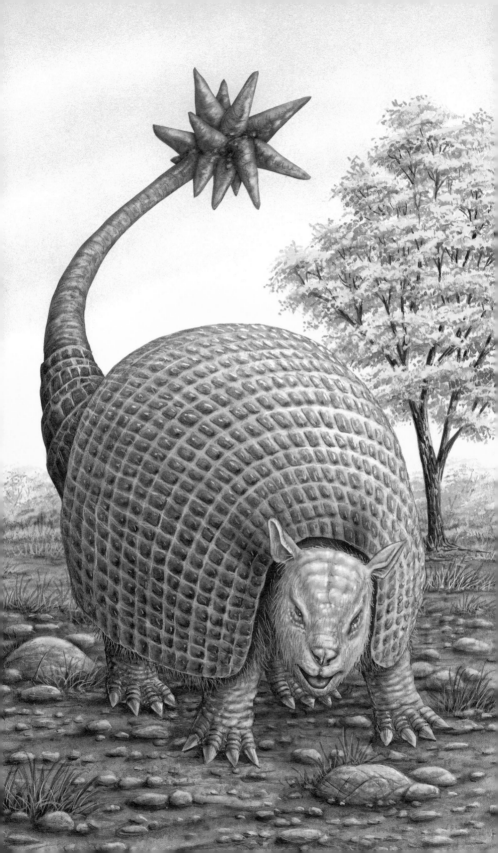

GLYPTODON

You say it like this:

GLIP-toe-don

The Glyptodon was the size

of a small car.

It was covered with bony

skin from head to tail.

Some glyptodons had a bony club

at the end of their tails.

They were not fast,

but they never had to run

away from anything.

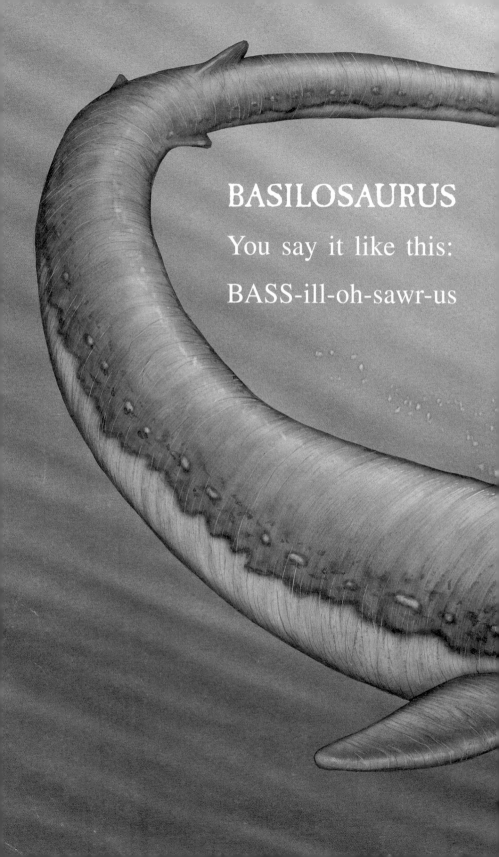

BASILOSAURUS

You say it like this:

BASS-ill-oh-sawr-us

Basilosaurus was
an early whale.
It looked a little like a sea serpent.
It had a long, thin body
and lots of sharp teeth.
It ate fish.

PLATYBELODON

You say it like this:

plat-ee-BELL-oh-don

Platybelodon was
as big as an elephant.

Its front teeth were
as big as shovels.
They were shaped
like shovels too!
Platybelodon dug
up plants to eat
with its shovel-like teeth.

HYRACOTHERIUM

You say it like this:

Hi-RACK-oh-THEER-ee-um

Hyracotherium was

the ancestor of all horses.

But it was much smaller

than the horses of today.

It was the size of a small dog.

It was too small to run fast.

It was too small to protect itself.

It had to hide

so it didn't get eaten.

ANDREWSARCHUS

You say it like this:

an-droo-SARK-us

Andrewsarchus had jaws
that were longer than your arm.

It had lots of strong teeth.

Andrewsarchus ate other animals.

It ate all the meat,

then it crushed the bones

and ate them, too!

MEGATHERIUM

You say it like this:
meg-ah-THEER-ee-um

Megatherium looked like
a bear with a big, fat tail
and very long claws.
But it was much, much
bigger than any bear.
Megatherium was
as tall as the treetops
when it stood on its back legs.
It ripped down high branches
to eat the leaves.

MACRAUCHENIA

You say it like this:

mak-raw-KEEN-ee-ah

The Macrauchenia looked like
three animals mixed together.
It had a body like a camel.
It had feet like a rhinoceros.
It had a short trunk,
like an elephant.
All of this put together
made one strange beast!

INDRICOTHERIUM

You say it like this:

in-DRIK-oh-THEER-ee-um

Indricotherium was the
largest land mammal ever.
It weighed more
than four elephants put together.
If Indricotherium was
still alive today,
it could peek into a second-story
window without stretching.
Now that is really big!

HOMO SAPIEN

You say it like this:

HO-mo SAPE-ee-in

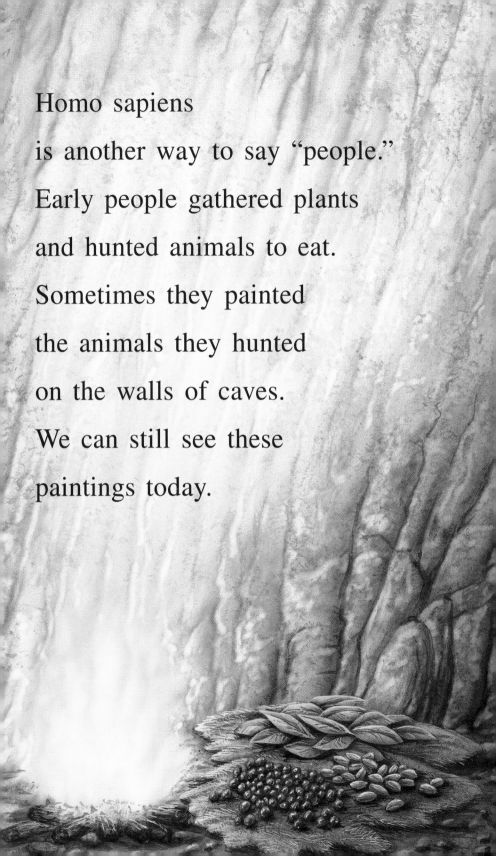

Homo sapiens
is another way to say "people."
Early people gathered plants
and hunted animals to eat.
Sometimes they painted
the animals they hunted
on the walls of caves.
We can still see these
paintings today.

Now people live
all over the earth.
But the other mammals
in this book are gone.
They died long ago.
Sometimes when they died
their bones were preserved.
These bones are called fossils.
Scientists study fossil bones
to learn about ancient mammals
and other prehistoric animals.

AUTHOR'S NOTE

The first mammals were small, nocturnal animals tha evolved over 200 million years ago, during the age of th dinosaurs. The mammals stayed small until 65 million yea ago, when the dinosaurs suddenly went extinct. With th dinosaurs gone, mammals began to evolve and grow bigge As time went by, newer mammals continued to evolve an older mammals became extinct. This book describes som of the most dramatic mammals known from the fossil recor Many of the animals shown here went extinct millions c years ago, but others survived until the end of the last ic age, approximately 11,000 years ago. These ice-age mamma include woolly mammoths, saber-toothed tigers, Glyptodo Megatherium, and Macrauchenia. Prehistoric humans wou have seen and hunted many of these animals during the la ice age. Cave paintings showing mammoths and other extinc animals date back to over 40,000 years ago.

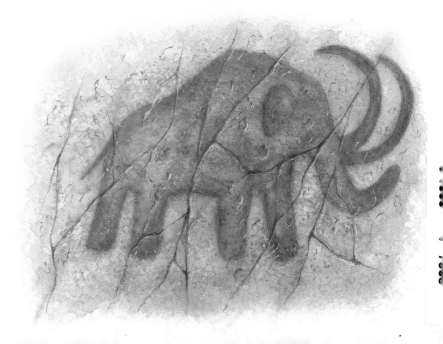